LET'S LOOK AT
Nature

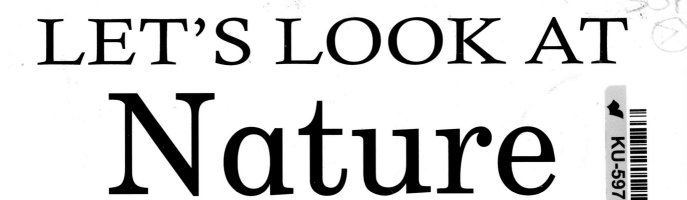

KU-597-163

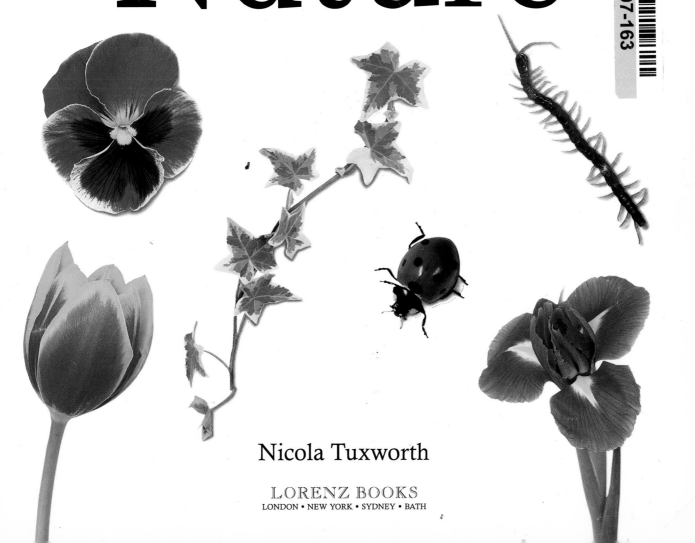

Nicola Tuxworth

LORENZ BOOKS
LONDON • NEW YORK • SYDNEY • BATH

Spring

Spring is the season when everything starts to grow.

Fluffy chicks are born...

...trees uncurl their leaves...

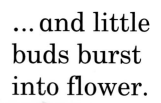

...and little buds burst into flower.

When there is crisp
snow on the ground...

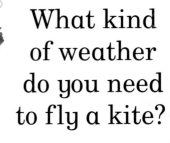

...do you like
to play with
snowballs?

What kind
of weather
do you need
to fly a kite?

In the garden

Flowers, birds, trees and insects live in gardens.

Do you like gardening?

fierce, stripey wasps

tall tulip

slender gladioli

purple iris

frilly carnation

slithery
snails

shiny blackbird

spotty
ladybird

Which kind of
flowers do
you like best?

scented
freesia

thorny
rose

In the forest

Animals, birds and insects live amongst the tall trees.

noisy woodpecker

nimble squirrel

prickly pine cone

feathery ferns

What can you see in this forest?

sleek
fox

shy rabbit

On the beach

Shells and seaweed
are washed up
on to the beach.

sandy
sea lion

noisy seagull

Have you ever seen a
crab scuttling sideways?

slippery
seaweed

tropical sandy beach

Some sea
creatures live
in shells.

Do you like
building
castles in
the sand?

Under the sea

Lots of amazing
plants and
creatures live
under the sea.

dangerous shark

spotty lobster

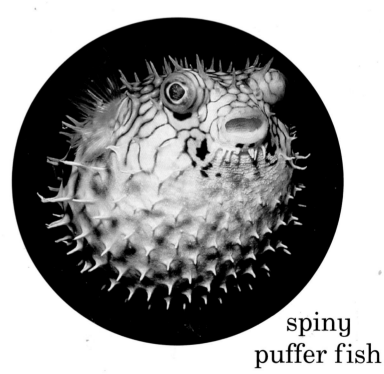

spiny
puffer fish

brittle, feathery coral

brightly striped tropical fish

Have you ever tried snorkelling in the sea?

Ponds

Lots of different plants and animals like to live in, or near, water.

waterlilies

lush, green pond

blotchy, brown frog

A shimmering stickleback swims about under the water.

gliding pond skater

Can you waddle like a duck?

darting dragonfly

Minibeasts

Minibeasts creep, crawl and scuttle everywhere.

creepy-crawly woodlice

wiggly worm

marching ants

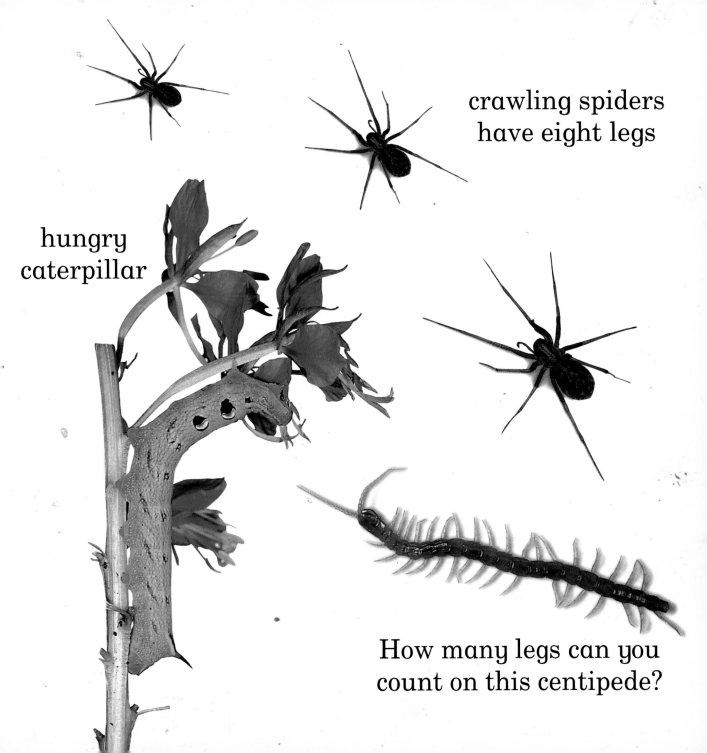

crawling spiders
have eight legs

hungry
caterpillar

How many legs can you
count on this centipede?

Can you remember where these things are found?

KU-395-034

Suddenly one day
he was standing in the yard.
Appeared out of nowhere.
Just stood there.
He had eyes and a nose and ears
just like everybody.
And yet he was not at all like anyone else.

"Hi," she said.
But he didn't answer.
"Hi!" she said again. But he still didn't answer.
"Can't you hear me?" she screamed,
angry as a bee, or a wasp. She was furious.

But he was silent.
He turned away.
He looked off in another
direction.

Then he left
just as suddenly as he had come.
Didn't even say goodbye to her.
Just turned around.
And disappeared.

But the next day he was back again.
Suddenly appeared. Just stood there.
And stared. Silent as an apple.
So she didn't say anything either.
Who did he think he was?
She wasn't going to talk to *him*!
Really stupid, that's what he was.
A dope. A dummy.
She didn't talk to people like that.
Certainly not!

But there were still swings to play on.
And as she swung back and forth a little,
he sat down on the railing.
Watching her.
Finally he climbed up onto another swing.
Making it swing in time with hers.
As if they belonged together,
even though they didn't belong together at all.

But that's what he did.
Although he didn't say a word.
As usual.

Anna Walfridson

The next day she waited for him,
even though he really wasn't worth
waiting for.
When would he come? she wondered.
Why didn't he come?
Why wasn't he suddenly standing there?
Silently.
Just standing there.

But no.
No one came that day.
Only Steve and Nabila and Carlos
and Rob and Judy
played with her in the playground.
But they didn't count.
They were there every day.
And they were totally different from the
silent boy.
The strange boy who was much too strange
for her to want to wait for him.
Even though she *had* started to wait …
No. Now
she would think about something else.

Then it was Saturday.
The rain poured down.
Then it was Sunday.
The rain poured down.
The swings sighed in the wind.
The jungle gym stood bare and naked.
Who would go outside in weather like this?
No one.
Definitely not her.

Until she saw him.
Near the fence.
Near the mound.
Near the little hill.
Then over by the sandbox,
where he sat down and stared straight ahead.
As if looking at nothing.

Quick, on with her jacket!
Hurry, on with her boots!
Fast as lightning over to the door.
But her mother said in surprise,
"Are you going outside?"
"Yes."
"Are you going out like that?"
"YES!"
"But why on earth?
And in weather like this!"

There was only one way to answer that.
"I have to."
And she repeated,
"I have to. I have to. I HAVE TO!"

Sometimes mothers don't understand anything.
Not one thing.
It's almost unbelievable
how unbelievably little they understand.

Luckily, there's something called stubbornness.
STUBBORNNESS!
Anyway, there she stood at last.
In the playground. In front of the sandbox.
In front of the boy sitting on the edge of the
sandbox.
"Hi."
"Hi."
He could talk! She was surprised,
even though she had suspected he could.

Time passed.
Seconds. Minutes. Hours.
How hard they worked!
How they dug and scooped, built and shaped,
designed and planted!
They transformed the playground into a
landscape.
Long, winding rivers twisted this way and that.
Bushes sprouted up.
Trees bent their branches.
Boats slowly chugged along.

Until it was time for her to eat.
Even though she didn't want to.
DIDN'T WANT TO.
But she had to:
"I'll be right back ..."

When she returned, he was gone.
The swings creaking.
The jungle gym deserted.
The slushy pool of the sandbox.
The rain still coming down.
The bushes bending over even farther.
The trees that had toppled.
And the boats, which she kicked far, far away.
Good riddance.

A week went by.
And then another.
Week after endless week.
Until it was the first day of school.
And there was the school and the school yard
and all the children.
And the bell rang to call them inside.

And there at a desk sat the boy.

But she didn't dare sit next to him.
Absolutely not.
So she sat down somewhere else.
Until she suddenly changed her mind,
and moved.
And she got up her courage
to sit at a desk right next to him.
"I'm going to sit next to you," she said.
"I want to sit next to you.
Yes, I think I'll sit here," she dared to say.

Even though the other girls giggled.
And all the boys started to laugh.
And the teacher smiled in that peculiar way
grownups sometimes do
when you really don't want them to smile.
She stayed where she was.
Stayed in her seat, that's all there was to it.
Their laughter couldn't chase her away.

But what about the boy?
Well, he stayed where he was, too.
As if he had never sat next to
anyone else.
Her place was next to his.
His place was next to hers.
That's the way it should be.

So they were allowed to sit there in peace.
No one laughed anymore.
No one giggled anymore.
(Although the teacher may have been smiling a tiny
bit, if you looked closely.)

All right,
now school could really begin.
One, two, three.
Then it was time to draw.
They were given crayons.
And paper.
A blank piece of paper, clean and white,
lay in front of each of them,
waiting.

That was when she decided.
She chose red.
She reached out
and took the red crayon
and drew a big heart.
The reddest one she could draw.
And the biggest.
It filled up the whole page.

And when she finished her drawing,
she looked up.
Looked at him.
Looked at his paper, too.
But he wasn't drawing anything.
And he didn't seem to know
what he wanted to draw.

Until she held up her drawing.
So that he would see it.
So that he would understand.
So that he, too,
made up his mind
just then.
And reached out his hand for the red crayon.

C3 371849 00 F3

WITHDRAWN FROM
NEWCASTLE LIBRARIES

Friendship

Newcastle upon
CITY LIBR

Please return or renew th'
Books can be renewed at '
12199   not overdue or

Due for return	Dur
.... PI...	

Siv W... ...... Walfridson

Su... ...e Day

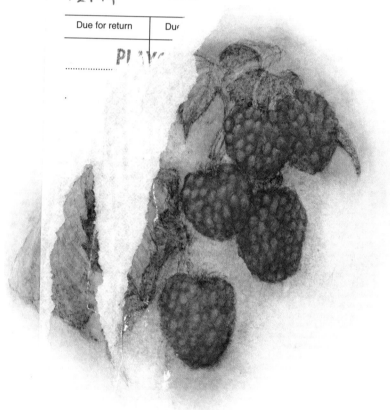

Translated by Tiina Nunnally

R&S
BOOKS

Stockholm   New York   London   Adelaide   Toronto

NEWCASTLE UPON TYNE
CITY LIBRARIES

Class No.	Acc. No.
JY	C337184900
Checked	Issued
H.W.	12|99

Rabén & Sjögren Stockholm

Translation copyright © 1993 by Rabén & Sjögren
All rights reserved
Originally published in Swedish by Rabén & Sjögren
under the title *Plötsligt en dag*, text copyright © 1991 by Siv Widerberg
Illustrations copyright © 1991 by Anna Walfridson
Library of Congress catalog card number: 93 661 CIP
Printed in Denmark
Aarhuus Stiftsbogtrykkerie
First edition, 1993

ISBN 91 29 622 48 4